Your Hurt Inner Child: Healing Childhood Trauma as an Adult

Kate Golinski

Published by Kate Golinski, 2023.

While every precaution has been taken in the preparation of this book, the publisher assumes no responsibility for errors or omissions, or for damages resulting from the use of the information contained herein.

YOUR HURT INNER CHILD: HEALING CHILDHOOD TRAUMA AS AN ADULT

First edition. November 27, 2023.

Copyright © 2023 Kate Golinski.

ISBN: 979-8223380429

Written by Kate Golinski.

Table of Contents

Introduction: The Beginnings of a Traumatized Child

*The wounds you have are not your fault. But they **are** your responsibility to heal.*

The path to healing begins by going inwards. The path forward, paradoxically, begins by going backward.

Inside of you, in all of us, is our inner child. Those who had a secure, nurturing upbringing connect with their inner child on a regular basis. After all, their inner child reminds them to seek out joy, new experiences, and playfulness. That was, for the most part, their childhood.

Those of us who endured a tumultuous, unstable, abusive, and traumatic childhood don't have the same relationship with our inner child. We don't check in with them, we don't tend to their needs, and we don't endeavor to make sure they feel safe. After all, we weren't ever afforded that from our caregivers (most likely parents, although this differs from situation to situation.) We don't know *how* to offer those things.

Plus, our inner child reminds us of upsetting events from our past. When we are made to feel incapable at work, it's our inner child who feels the shame and embarrassment. It regurgitates the same feelings we felt when our parents - in my case, my mother - told us we were stupid.

When our feelings toward another person aren't reciprocated, it's our inner child that feels the stabbing pain of rejection: the same all-consuming rejection we felt as a child when we were made to feel like an unwanted burden.

We find ourselves feeling guilt and shame for simply *being*; the same guilt and shame we harbored as a child when we were made to feel unlovable.

Your hurt inner child is silently hurting from all of the emotional pain and trauma they endured growing up. You carried that with you as you grew up. Now's the time to delve into the past, understand the anguish and trauma you hold inside of you, and rescue the scared child within.

Many of us spend so much of our energy trying to suppress and block out traumatic memories and events that occurred during childhood that we eventually lose sight of who we are. When we do this, we bury our inner child - which is a key component of us. When we grow up, we don't leave our inner child like a caterpillar growing out of its cocoon. We bring our inner child with us.

I buried my inner child. For three decades, I neglected my hurt inner child. For the most part, I did this to avoid facing the pain of past events. The other reason was that I just had no idea where to start when comforting my traumatized inner child.

Before we go any further, I'd like to tell you a little of my story. Maybe yours is similar, or you find aspects of mine run parallel to yours. Maybe my childhood - clouded by an emotionally abusive mother and alcoholic father - isn't something you can relate to.

But, the reason you've chosen this book is the same reason I sought out books like this in my 30s: because of trauma suffered as a child. Not only that, I'd grown up neglecting my wounded inner child and found myself in a place of perpetual heartbreak and sadness. I wanted to fix that.

No matter what broke you as a child: an unstable home, violence, narcissistic parents, being made into the "black sheep" of the family, emotional abuse, or any of the other thousands of ways hurtful adults break innocent children, your adult self can't be fixed until the inner child is. You are one and the same.

My story began in the early 80s. I was born into a tumultuous environment with an unreliable, alcoholic father and a mother whom I could never make happy. As far back as I can remember, my mother hated spending time with me. She didn't play with me like I saw other moms playing with their kids. She didn't speak to me in a playful manner like I saw the other moms do. Half of the time, she was hurtful and unkind to me. The other half, I could tell she was only taking care of me because she had to. While offering some love, my father was inconsistent and scary. His temper was unpredictable and violent, his rages mostly reserved for my mother.

As an adult, I can now see my mother was depressed, anxious, and forever on eggshells due to my father's mood swings and changeability. While I sympathize with this, and I find myself pitying the dire situation she was in (which I too was in, although I didn't choose to be), I've always found it hard to sympathize with her feeling it was acceptable to call me stupid, pointless, difficult to be around, and undeserving. I have deep, deep empathy for anybody suffering with their mental health. I also struggled with my own for years, so I understand it.

But, her cruel treatment of me wasn't wholly down to her inner turmoil. She could bite her tongue if other people were around, and she knew not to be mean in front of other mothers at the school gates. She could contain herself, which shows she could help herself from treating me so poorly. This means her cruelty toward me was intentional.

As for my father, his violent outbursts and drunken slumbers were actually easier to deal with than the abuse I suffered at the hands of my mother. I learned ways to deal with him, such as pouring him a double when he told me to get him a drink. That way, I knew he'd pass out quicker, and perhaps we could survive the night without something angering him.

While he was violent, he was somehow the more gentle parent. A paradoxical statement, I know, but growing up in an abusive household isn't black and white. We can have parents who simultaneously hurt us yet are the ones to offer us comfort.

As I said, your childhood may have been similar to this, or it may not. Still, if you endured abuse, trauma, or mistreatment at the hands of your parents or caregivers, there's a high likelihood you harbor a wounded inner child. If that's the case, I hope this book can go some way in helping you understand and work to overcome your trauma.

I've walked this road myself and know how daunting it is. Let me offer guidance on your journey and help you reach your hurt inner child. Only then can healing begin.

Chapter 1: Understanding the Inner Child

Every time I hear someone raising their voice, I regress into six-year-old me.

In this chapter, I want to cover three things: what an inner child is, signs you have an unhealed inner child, and why you need to reconnect with them in order to heal from traumas.

You may have noticed I began this section with a quote. For each chapter of this book, I'll start with a quote that may resonate with you. These quotes make you think, prompt introspection, and allow you to be at a place where you're ready to accept the guidance this book will offer.

The quote, *every time I hear someone raising their voice, I regress into six-year-old me,* was something I read online years ago from someone describing the after-effects of childhood trauma. It stopped me in my tracks. It perfectly described something I had felt for so long but had been unable to put into words so succinctly. This quote was one of the first that triggered something in me to delve into researching inner children and the ways trauma shapes us. I hope the quotes throughout this book will help ignite your desire to heal.

Our inner child is every iteration of us. You as a baby, toddler, child, young adult... It's every version of yourself that has existed before adulthood. It's an ever-present, though often ignored, aspect of all of us.

The inner child remembers everything you've been through. They remember the things you heard, the things you saw, and the experiences you had that traumatized and disturbed you. They remember the heartbreak of rejection, the pain of grief, and the fear of doing "something wrong."

Our inner child remembers how it felt to be the last one picked to be on a team. They remember the stinging feeling of holding back tears when they were scolded by a parent. They remember the last time they saw Grandma, not realizing it would be the last time. In a nutshell, our inner child embodies every feeling we had growing up. Not just the bad ones - the good ones are there, too.

My inner child remembers the powdery scent of my nana's blusher. The comfort of the hot water bottle on a winter's night. The feeling of being allowed to play video games all day on a rainy Sunday. The overwhelming smell of paint from my grandad's shed on a summer's day. If you think back, you'll be able to find some light amidst the darkness, too.

It goes to show that our inner child is always connecting and communicating with us, although we rarely pay them much heed. Particularly when they evoke uncomfortable feelings, such as reminding us of awful memories triggering our flight response or taking us back to the time we were six years old and being yelled at by a parent. We want to bury those things. We never want to experience them again. We suppress, ignore, and sometimes even whitewash our own traumatic experiences so that we don't have to face them.

A big part of the journey to healing your inner child is listening to them, but we'll get to that later. As it stands, even while you may be ignoring your inner child, they're still controlling your thoughts and actions. They don't want you to feel shame, pain, embarrassment or rejection. So, when you say no to social events, hide away from situations outside of your comfort zone, or react emotionally to criticism, it's your inner child reacting. All they want is to keep you safe. They're a child; they don't understand they're keeping you in the same cycle of trauma. All they know is they're protecting you.

Now would be a good time to consider times when your inner child has been the dictator of your behavior. Have you stopped yourself from speaking up about something for fear of sounding "stupid"? Have you avoided sticking up for yourself when you ought to for fear of rebuttal? Have there been occasions where you let people treat you unfairly, but you simply endure it because you somehow feel you must "deserve" poor treatment?

Take a few moments to consider times like this where it's not the adult you calling the shots; it's your wounded inner child. The more you think, the more instances you can likely conjure up. When I thought about this for the first time, I was shocked at how little "grown-up me" was controlling my own behavior. My traumatized inner child was doing their best to stop us from hurting anymore, and I was simply a passenger. Of course, I didn't realize this at the time. But looking back, the unconscious beliefs that were implanted during my childhood were navigating me through life.

And, since our adult self and child self don't have a relationship, how can our inner child know that we don't need to be so hyper-vigilant anymore? That we have more power, more control, and full autonomy? That the protective measures they have in place are actually holding us back?

Every bit of trauma, emotional turmoil, and every instance of terror and panic you felt as a child is still within you, and you don't need me to tell you it's one tough burden to carry. Reconnecting with your inner child is imperative for healing and becoming the person you should have been.

Before I cover the signs of a wounded inner child, I'd like to remind you of some of the life-changing benefits of inner child work.

It can help reduce your overall anxiety.

It can help regulate your emotional responses to events and situations, i.e., keep your response proportionate to the situation.

It helps you learn to be more gentle with yourself.

It can help you in your relationships. The walls and barriers come down, enabling you to receive love and kindness without guilt or overthinking.

It helps you make more mature and self-serving decisions (which does not equate to selfishness).

It can help us recognize self-sabotaging behaviors and quash them.

It will reconnect you with your enthusiastic, curious, and energetic self that looks at the world with a sense of wonder.

It teaches you to self-parent - an important aspect of healing when we weren't always parented the way we needed to be when we were younger.

Once we cultivate a safe space for our inner child, we can bloom. We need to abolish the thought that child-you and adult-you have to react the same. We just need to show our inner child this.

Since you've picked up this book and read this far, I will guess that you're confident you need to engage in some inner child work. In case you are unsure, I'll cover some signs of a wounded inner child. Before I do, let me explain what a healthy inner child looks like.

A healthy, happy inner child doesn't worry about molding themself to make others happy. While they show compassion and concern for others, they won't bend to uncomfortable positions to appease others. They have boundaries that they enforce because they feel comfortable and confident enough to say "no." They don't fear things outside of their knowledge or comfort zone but rather feel exhilarated at the idea of opportunity. They feel able to deal with and get through difficult times in life without retreating or engaging in harmful coping mechanisms.

A wounded inner child simply can't comprehend living life so full of self-assurance. Let me explain the adult symptoms of a hurt inner child.

1. You engage in self-criticism and suffer with low self-esteem

Those with a traumatized inner child will often speak to themselves poorly. The inner critic is a toxic, hate-spewing goblin that makes sure any self-compassion or kindness is stomped out immediately. "You're too stupid to apply for that job," "If you walk past that crowd of people, they'll look at you and laugh," "The barista forgot the milk in your coffee - don't speak up, you'll annoy them."

These low vibrational thoughts aren't yours - they aren't even really your inner child's - they're the result of being spoken to and treated poorly as a child. They're the outcome of being hurt so badly by your caregiver that you've developed unconscious beliefs about yourself. Few of them are good. Most of them are self-condemning. Your inner child serves as your messenger for these thoughts because that's what younger you was conditioned to believe: that you were unworthy. Unimportant. A burden. That your feelings had to be suppressed and not vocalized. That you were stupid.

Does your inner critic sabotage you rather than serve you? We all have some form of inner critic, but the main difference between a healthy and an unhealthy one is how we speak to ourselves. A healthy inner critic will be constructive, compassionate, and kind. Does yours lean more toward a toxic inner critic?

2. Small things evoke big emotions

A lot of the time, we suppress and "forget" the traumas we endured as a child. It's been known to take people hours upon hours of therapy to begin remembering the most horrific, traumatic things they endured as children simply because they'd buried them so deep they couldn't remember them. What they did remember, though, was how that trauma made them feel. While they forgot the event itself, the inner child remembered the feeling of the event.

As I mentioned, your adult behavior is often navigated by your inner child. If you find that your reactions to certain situations or actions of others tend to be excessive or disproportionate, it could be your hurt inner child causing that to surface.

For example, you may get angry and frustrated when someone talks over you during a conversation. Granted, it's entirely bad manners to interrupt or talk over someone. But we all know people who do it, and we can process that behavior as bad behavior on their part. It's a "*them* problem," not something that reflects poorly on us. However, if you find yourself getting irate and full of rage at someone doing this, and it consumes you that someone felt able to disrespect you like this, then it may be due to being ignored or unheard as a child.

What you have to say or what you need was disregarded or not considered. When we come across something similar in adulthood, like being talked over or unheard in conversation, it triggers our inner child's needs being unmet. It's a feeling we've had before, and we hate it - it reinforces that we're not worthy or deserving of attention.

Other things, like people being late or never being on time, someone not texting you back, or someone falling through on a promise, may evoke feelings of anger and rage. It's your inner child, your past pain, provoking this extreme reaction from you. The examples I've outlined above, in the grand scheme of things, are trivial. Annoying, yes, inconsiderate, yes... but they aren't malicious or willfully cruel. Our inner child can certainly view it that way, though.

Strong responses to minor events suggest the inner child needs you to tend to them.

3. You engage in self-sabotaging behaviors

Have you ever begun snarking at your partner or a person close to you to provoke an argument for no reason? Or find yourself being late to work despite being warned about this already? Perhaps you find yourself scrolling social media rather than doing that accounting you've been putting off? These are all examples of self-sabotage.

But why would your hurt inner child want to sabotage your opportunities and happiness? Fear and anxiety. Remember, your hurt inner child believes they're unworthy, incapable, undeserving, and certain to fail. You can't lose if you don't enter the competition in the first place, right?

This applies to most aspects of adult life. Relationships, career, personal development, and finances are all seen as a source of fear. You may find you've sabotaged relationships in the past after engaging in behavior that caused it to end, despite being truly fond of your partner. You've perhaps talked yourself out of applying for a job, rationalizing why it's not a good fit for you when really you're fearful of "rejection." It's amazing how much we can logicize thoughts that are actually self-sabotaging.

The fearful child in us is doing their best to stop us from feeling any more pain.

4. You dissociate to get by

We all have coping mechanisms. Like all life strategies, they come in both good and bad variants. Our inner child, again doing their best to help us avoid feeling past traumas, tends to offer some pretty unhealthy coping mechanisms. Bear in mind, these are the same techniques that younger you used to deal with the hurtful events and situations you endured. As an adult, you no longer need these mechanisms; they can be replaced with healthy, healing mechanisms. Still, the fearful inner child needs to be convinced of this.

One big coping mechanism we often utilize is dissociation. This means we disconnect from the world around us, from the situation we're in, or from what we're doing. This mental shift can make us feel like we're actually detached from our body like we're no longer in our physical vessel. Things feel unreal - it can make us feel extremely panicked and surreal. We switch into autopilot and become the passenger.

It's our minds' way of coping with stress and trauma. I recall when I first felt dissociation as a child. It felt otherworldly; I had no idea what was happening, and it was scary. When I looked at my feet beneath me, it was almost as if I didn't recognize them as my own. I was there in body but certainly not in spirit. The first time this happened, I was sitting on the staircase as my father beat my mother in the living room. It had happened multiple times before, the screams of my mother making me sick to my stomach, but as a five-year-old girl, I was powerless to help. This time, to help me deal with the situation, I dissociated.

It wasn't intentional. I didn't will myself to do it. My five-year-old brain had no other preservation techniques other than to disconnect me from the horror I was in.

The ability to dissociate stayed with me as I grew. In fact, it still appears here and there when I'm encountering life's stresses - but now I'm a healthier person than I was for the first three and a half decades of my life, and I can calmly bring myself out of it.

Is this something that happens to you? If so, when does it begin, and can you find its triggers? Almost all of the time, the answer lies in childhood.

5. You struggle with relationship issues

There's a correlation between traumatized, hurt people attracting narcissistic, abusive individuals. That's not to say every wounded person is prey for or susceptible to the clutches of an abuser but hurt people have traits that abusive people seek out. Those of us who have been through upsetting, traumatic events are often full of empathy and forgiveness for others. This is like hitting the jackpot for an abuser.

We give second chances. We often don't have a healthy, true view of ourselves. We love hard. We accept poor treatment because that's what we've learned to endure.

Have you been in toxic, abusive partnerships, or do you find yourself in a pattern of fleeing them only to enter another? Perhaps you try to "fix" people whom you see the good in, ignoring the red flags as you do. Or, you might chase and fight for someone who wouldn't notice if you fell off the face of the earth. These are all symptoms of a broader attachment issue caused by childhood experiences.

My first two serious relationships were marred by physical and emotional abuse. I was almost 30 when I realized that not every relationship has aggression behind closed doors. I thought it was a secret we all kept because we loved our spouses, and you worked through these things. Can you imagine three whole decades of thinking that way? I was ashamed of this, but when it's all you know, how can you know there's anything different out there?

6. You deal with mental, emotional, and physical issues

Trauma rears its head in many ways. You may already know (and be feeling the effects) of trauma-induced mental and emotional issues. But trauma can cause physical problems, too. The body stores the damage other people cause, and it can manifest in ways that affect our body. It can trigger fatigue (fibromyalgia has been linked to trauma suffered in childhood), migraines, and stomach problems. Not to mention the racing heart and sweating we can develop when feeling something close to an unwanted childhood feeling.

Naturally, both mental and physical issues can be debilitating. PTSD can leave us feeling utterly hopeless and drowning. When we aren't in bouts of panic and anxiety, we can revert to feeling numb and empty. I know when I was suffering badly with my anxiety, I told a friend that all I wanted to feel was nothing. I didn't want to be happy, I just wanted to be nothing. I couldn't deal with the rollercoaster of emotions; I wanted off the ride and simply spectate. I couldn't deal with life.

In reality, and unbeknown to me, I was leaving it up to my inner child to deal with life. Of course they couldn't handle it. They were just doing what they thought was best, and their infant way of coping was destroying me. My inner child was trying to communicate with me, and I was letting them flounder, which, in turn, caused me to struggle.

Chapter 2: Childhood Trauma and Self-Perception

It's an overwhelming thought to think of how many broken children are suffering inside adult bodies.

You took on so much and carried so many emotional burdens as a child, ones you never should have had to carry. The main purpose of this book is to guide you to release yourself from that traumatic weight holding you down. But first, I want to help you understand the trauma you endured, how that shaped your inner child, and thus the perception you have of yourself as an adult.

Trauma can be buried deep. We sometimes need guidance when processing what we endured and fully accepting what we went through. I'll discuss the variations of abuse we can endure as children, and you can see which variant you were exposed to. It may be one variant; it may be them all: trauma is trauma. We all have different experiences of it, but they tend to all boil down to these categories.

First off is **physical abuse**. Hitting, harming, shaking, grabbing with the intent to hurt... basically any possible scenario whereby the adult physically harms the child intentionally. This is usually the caregiver, but it can be other family members, people known to the family, or individuals entrusted to care for the child.

We live in an age now where physical abuse of a child is punishable by law. I recall growing up, our teachers were able to reprimand students by forcibly dragging them to the detention area. Our neighbors up the road would punish their children by hitting them. These kids were often seen with bruises on their arms or sometimes their faces. In fact, I once saw the matriarch of this family slap her daughter for asking for takeout for tea as they walked past our backyard. My mother saw this, too, but didn't do anything. Bystanders saw. Nobody did anything.

Thankfully, we live in an age now where this woman would be punished for her actions. This was the early 90s, though, and hitting your kids was another one of those things that people chose to ignore. Certainly, it was in the area I grew up in. Although not exactly the "wrong side of the tracks," the place was rife with people living by their own laws.

This woman's children grew up and went no contact with her. I bet the mother now proclaims she has "no idea why" her kids avoid having anything to do with her.

My point is there are so many adults who suffered abuse due to it being "acceptable" at the time. Now, they have to try to heal their deep-seated wounds.

Children who experienced physical abuse tend to suffer from adulthood depression and anxiety and are prone to PTSD. Being hit or put in harm's way as a child is confusing, frightening, and creates a breeding ground for adulthood mental health problems.

Another source of childhood trauma is **sexual abuse**. The mere idea of this kills me, let alone knowing it goes on in the world. Such evil, and the people who let it happen, ought to have no place among us. I say *the people who let it happen* because I believe they're just as bad as the perpetrators. It reminds me of that quote: the only thing evil needs is for good men to do nothing.

I wasn't exposed to sexual abuse, although I did manage to flee the clutches of some predators, which is traumatizing in itself. However, I managed to fight my way out of these bad situations and get myself to safety. Too many children can't, either through freezing out of fear, being too young to know what was happening, or trusting their abuser. Sometimes, the child feels too guilty to fight back or speak up. Fear of being "exposed" and "shamed" is also a big component in a child having no voice.

The quote at the beginning of this book, *the wounds you have are not your fault. But they are your responsibility to heal,* frustrated me so much when I first heard it. It's maddening because it's true. *But someone else caused these awful wounds and traumas - they should pay for that! That would fix me,* were thoughts that would consume me.

I can imagine, if you've endured sexual abuse, that you feel bouts of anger, bitterness, and unjustness like this. Anger is part of the healing process, although most people often get stuck on that step without moving on. I can understand why, but if that sounds like you, I need to implore you to keep the above quote in mind. Nothing that happened to you was ever your fault, and the internal wounds you carry aren't things you need to feel guilt or shame over. Somebody else did this to you, but you are responsible for the healing.

When we let unfairness, the lack of justice, or the absence of karma consume us, we're keeping ourselves trapped in the cycle of trauma. I've been bitter, I've been engulfed in blame, and I've even spent many a night contemplating revenge on those who've wronged me. It took me a while to realize that the only person this was hurting was me. An eye for an eye does make the whole world blind. I do, though, have faith that people who do wrong get their just deserts, whether we're there to see it or not.

I'd also like to stress that sexual abuse doesn't always have to be physical, either. It can come in the form of being made to watch inappropriate (read: adult) movies. It could come in the form of indecent exposure. It can come in vulgar language. Abuse isn't black and white like so many people think it is.

Children exposed to this type of abuse can go on to harm themselves, engage in reckless behavior, and turn to drugs and alcohol to help them cope. And it goes without saying they struggle with adult relationships, particularly romantic ones.

A lesser-covered but just as prevalent form of childhood abuse is **emotional abuse**. In fact, it's the most common form of abuse toward children, but there's a much greater tolerance for it (historically, at least. I'm aware times have changed since you and I were children).

I remember my friend saying to me when we were teenagers, "I'd rather my mother hit me instead of treating me that way." My friend's mother would belittle her, find any little thing to scold her for and withhold affection from her. "All I've ever done is try to love her, and she hates me," my friend told me. She had no idea I felt the same about my own mother - I kept everything inside and never told anyone my problems. My mother instilled that into me, making sure if I was talking too much as a child (i.e., revealing too much about what was going on behind closed doors), I'd get a sharp nip to the back of my arm. As I grew up, I just kept my problems to myself.

But my friend's passing comment about preferring to be hit over discarded got me thinking. I mean, no child should ever have to endure either, but my friend didn't see a world in which that would be an option. So, out of the two options available, physical or emotional pain, she would choose physical.

I think this shows just how much her mother's treatment of her affected her. A punch in the face is preferable to the silent treatment. A shove to the floor would be chosen over name-calling. A kick to the legs seemed a better option than not knowing what mood mom would be in when you got back home.

My mother would stop talking to me for days if I did something to upset her. As a young child, I'd plead and beg her to talk to me. I'd cry, sob, and tug at her trouser leg, just wanting to be picked up and told everything was okay. That I wasn't an "awful child." That I was too loved to be ignored. That my childlike infraction wasn't deserving of such cold, harsh treatment. As I got older, and after learning this didn't really work, I simply endured the days of coldness. She would stop washing my clothes. My meals were placed in the microwave for me to reheat instead of getting an invite to the dinner table. The only thing that would snap her out of it, aside from the passing of time, was if we had guests around. She'd quickly converse with me then.

As well as silent treatment, emotional abuse can be cruel words, narcissistic abuse (a whole world of pain for the victim, and perhaps a big enough topic for another book entirely), and emotional neglect. Then, you weave in the complexity of gaslighting, manipulation, guilt-tripping, intimidation, and threats. Unlike a bruise or scar, emotional abuse is harder to prove than physical abuse.

Often, the abuser will accuse the victim of exaggerating, taking things the wrong way, or being "too sensitive." When it's a child against an adult in this situation, often the child doesn't know how to vocalize such abuse or put it articulately enough to be understood. This enables the abuser to continue with their toxic treatment of the child.

Children who had to endure emotional abuse grow up with a poor sense of self and a negative self-image. They are doubtful of their capabilities and are likely to develop anxiety and depression. Quite literally, childhood abuse rewires a child's brain. Our formative years are so crucial in how we see ourselves and the world around us. Emotional abuse distorts both, altering our brains detrimentally.

This can be undone with a lot of work and introspection.

I feel like another less-covered source of childhood trauma is **family dysfunction**. This is an umbrella term for family conflict, a parent or parents who have substance problems, domestic abuse, violent siblings, an acrimonious divorce, or a parent who gets in trouble with the law. It also refers to a home where the caregivers have mental health issues. Household dysfunction is a trauma I can absolutely understand. What ought to be your safe space, your sanctuary, and your place of comfort is your personal hell.

My father was violent. He also struggled with his mental health, and was on various antipsychotics from his mid-40s until his death. Sometimes, even when he was on his medication, he would see things that weren't there. Naturally, as a child, this frightened me. I thought the things he was "seeing" were really there, and I was unable to see them. From seeing men with their arms chopped off in our living room to thinking my toy dragon was real, witnessing his fear truly terrified me.

There was no relief from this for me. I'd go to school, often in a state of panic and shock at the things I'd witnessed the night before, only to go home and see and hear even more disturbing things. Ironically, alcohol helped him stop hallucinating. It also sent him into deep slumbers, which meant a few hours of peace for me and my mother. I'd sneakily top up his whiskey or vodka (he'd change his drink of choice when one made him too ill) and wait for him to slump over so I could go to bed and not panic about bad things happening while I slept.

I couldn't possibly condense all of the years' worth of trauma I endured into one section of this book, but you'll likely understand the negative effects his mental struggles had on me. If you grew up in a dysfunctional household, you'll know the long-term effects are far-reaching. From an easy startle reflex, panicked reaction to loud noises or loud people, and general hypervigilance, it's hard for us to truly ever be calm and relaxed. For example, do you ever find you're doing something on autopilot - say watching TV - and you suddenly realize your shoulders are tense, pulled all the way up, and your posture is stiff and rigid? Even when you should be at your most relaxed, you never really are.

The next source of childhood trauma is **neglect**. Neglect isn't always what you see on the news or on soap operas, where neglected children are starved and left home alone for days on end (although, sadly, this happens more than we realize). It can be much more covert and harder to spot.

It's failing to get the child proper medical treatment. It's caregivers not feeding the child adequately or appropriately. It's failing to provide the child with warm clothing, shoes that fit, and a coat when the temperatures are freezing. There are two types of negligence: emotional and physical.

Emotional negligence is where the caregiver (I'm aware of the irony of using this term in this instance since care is scarcely given) withholds interactions. Physical negligence is putting the child in dangerous situations, refusing medical care when needed, and causing the child to suffer due to malnutrition.

As you can imagine, a child who grew up with an emotionally neglectful parent can have poor social and academic skills. They were never spoken to with love, never taught basic things, and weren't guided in their emotional development. This is hard - but not impossible - to undo in adulthood.

The final trigger of childhood trauma isn't at the hands of a caregiver but of other children. **Bullying** at the hands of your peers can cause great amounts of stress and anxiety. I say the caregiver or parent isn't to blame for this one, but sometimes they have their part to play here, too. For example, if you were getting bullied and sought help from your parents but were told to "toughen up" or "deal with it," this would no doubt leave you feeling helpless and unsupported.

Bullying can be hurtful, persistent name-calling, physical attacks, constant tormenting, and having rumors spread about you. It can be alienation, mind games, and, more recently, cyberbullying.

A child who endured bullying grows into an adult with poor self-worth, a toxic inner voice, and can often be highly sensitive. It can also cause the adult to live a life of anger and resentment, unable to let anybody in for fear of being hurt. Bullying and post-traumatic stress have been linked.

I wasn't necessarily bullied at school, but my home life made me withdrawn and insular. This made it difficult for me to make friends, so I was somewhat of a loner. However, for years, I would have flashbacks of the times we'd been asked to "pair up" in class and the knot that would develop in my stomach because I knew no one would pick me. I can only imagine the intense stress, trauma, and anxiety that full-blown bullying triggers.

For those who endured a rough time at school, they can sometimes find that this filters into the workplace, too. Sadly, some adults never grow out of their high school self, and their snarky, cliquey behavior seeps into their "grown up" life. Adults can find themselves traumatized by co-workers who target them and make their work life hell. While that goes beyond the scope of this book, I do wonder how unhappy these people must be to be so cruel and toxic to others.

Those six triggers of trauma aren't conclusive - like I say, trauma and the instigators of it aren't black and white. But, generally speaking, childhood trauma will fall into one or more of those categories. Hopefully, you can pinpoint where your childhood trauma stemmed from and are able to trace back the beginnings of your inner child being hurt. Now would be a good time to have a ten-minute introspection and consider some of the events and situations you went through that fall within these six categories:

Physical abuse

Sexual abuse

Emotional abuse

Family dysfunction

Neglect

Bullying

Delve into your past and remember how these events made you feel and how that correlates with your adult behavior. I'll come back to this in the next chapter, but this little exercise will help you find the invisible rope you have connecting you and your inner child. Once you're ready, we can pick up where we left off.

Are you ready to pick things up? Great! I know introspective dives into trauma can be something you want to resist, but it's an important part of the healing process. Please know that it does get easier.

As well as wanting to help you understand the sources of childhood trauma, I also wanted to cover how that manifests in our adulthood perception of ourselves. More specifically, I want to talk about self-esteem.

Self-esteem encapsulates our self-perception, self-understanding, and self-worth. These things navigate our actions, our thoughts, our feelings, and our worth. When we endure childhood trauma, our self-esteem develops to be incorrect and inaccurate in its estimation of ourselves.

We aren't born with built-in self-perception. We don't have an ingrained, perfectly accurate view of the world as soon as we enter it. These things are developed in childhood by our parents, caregivers, and the surroundings in which we grow up. If we're brought up around chaos, instability, put-downs, neglect, mistreatment, and forced to endure traumatic events, our self-perception is understandably skewed.

Those we depend on to nurture us and provide safety and comfort are the ones who play the biggest role in our self-esteem development. Be it parents, family members, school teachers, or other authority figures, these people mold how we view the world and our place in it.

If our early experiences with these individuals are traumatic, it damages our ability to accurately assess who we are. Poor self-esteem causes shame, guilt, and chronic self-loathing to fester within us and creates a perfect place for depression to thrive. It's a vicious cycle, all born from our childhood trauma.

Let me go over the symptoms of low self-esteem and how that ties in with early experiences.

Almost all of us who have endured a toxic upbringing can attest to **never feeling good enough**. No matter how hard we try, how much we want something, or how much we will ourselves to be better, we always end up feeling inadequate. Be it in relationships, at work, or just in life in general, we're in a perpetual state of feeling less than. Less than our peers, our co-workers, our relatives, and even comparing ourselves to people on TV in an unfavorable way.

We're not pretty enough, not clever enough, not witty enough, not interesting enough... The list can likely go on. Most of these beliefs are things either directly said to you during childhood or implied through your caregiver's actions. Naturally, if you're made to feel these things as a child, it can be hard to rewire your core belief system. You know already, if it was so easy to wipe our toxic beliefs clean and start again, we'd do it. It takes work, but too many damaged people are so broken from their traumas that they simply don't think it's possible.

Nothing I did would ever be good enough for my mother. From tidying my bedroom to the presents I got her for Christmas, I always seemed to mess up somewhere or fall short. I'd offer to clean my room all over again or exchange the gifts I'd got her, but the damage had been done. I'd disappointed her. Yet again, I'd failed despite trying so hard not to.

Over time, these repeated "failures" of mine chipped away at me. I began to realize not only that I frequently disappointed my mother but also that anything I did simply wasn't good enough. This spilled over into almost every other aspect of my young life and followed me into adulthood.

Another common symptom of low self-esteem is something called **self-erasure**. This sees us bury our authentic selves in order to make others happy. We'll undermine our own wants and needs to make sure other people's wants and needs are met. We'll people-please to the point where we don't value our own thoughts or opinions enough to voice them. If we did, we run the risk of upsetting someone or making them dislike us. *And we can't bear for that to happen.*

This is especially common if you found you were the "parent" in your relationship with your caregiver. If you were given adult responsibilities as a child, such as having to take care of siblings, take care of the home, or look after a parent, self-erasure is more prominent. In this instance, as well as the child's needs being unmet, they had to meet the needs of their caregiver. This double blow of trauma equates to a people-pleasing adult who neglects to tend to their own needs and wants.

Self-erasure also causes the adult to be unsure of their own desires, have poor self-care abilities, and find it difficult to say "no."

Poor self-care is also a whole symptom of its own when it comes to the adult effects of childhood trauma. We didn't feel an abundance of love as children, so how do we know how to offer it to ourselves as adults? Self-care isn't just bubble baths and hair masks - though it can be - it's taking an active role in protecting your own well-being and happiness.

Then there's **social anxiety**. Other people's thoughts of us can often sit at the forefront of our minds. When we enter a room, pass a group of people, or are introduced to a person for the first time, we often get overwhelmed with thoughts of how they perceive us. We often find that we're highly sensitive to others' opinions of us: *do they think we're weird? They looked at me "funny", they must think I'm ugly. I didn't look them in the eye enough when we spoke; they will think I'm weak.*

These thoughts bounce around our minds, much like they did when we were a child, trying to appease and please those around us. *Did I do the right thing? What if I didn't? Did I seem grateful enough for my birthday gift? I didn't smile enough when guests were here; they'd think I was miserable.*

The nervous, people-pleasing child becomes an adult who seeks validation and "good" opinions from others. This leads to social anxiety, with the idea of disapproval causing us to descend into dysfunction.

The detrimental effects of childhood trauma on our self-esteem will continue to plague us unless we find our wounded inner child, and that's what I want to cover next.

Chapter 3: Reconnecting with Little You

How would you take care of little you if you could parent them?

In this chapter, I want to cover the reasons why it's important to reconnect with your inner child and show you some techniques you can use to do this. I also want to guide you in revisiting childhood memories. I know so many of us bury and suppress anxieties and traumas that we can heal - if we'd only confront them.

Before we delve in, I just want you to think about the above quote for a few moments. If you were your parent, how would you take care of your younger self? There, of course, is no right or wrong answer. The way you answer this question, though, becomes another piece of the path that leads to healing.

I'm going to cover three reasons why you need to connect with your inner child. The benefits are far greater than you'd expect, so let me lay them out for you.

First of all, reconnecting with your inner child - often referred to as "inner child work" by professionals - is a great way for you to **become more self-aware**. True self-awareness is something those with a traumatized inner child simply don't have. When we begin to explore parts of ourselves that we've stuffed away and blocked out of view, it's like a whole new us is born. It's an enlightening experience.

We come to realize that it's not the grown-up us who is scared to say "no" to requests, who fears upsetting others, and who allows the opinions of others to consume us. It's our inner child. When we come to realize that we have the power to set boundaries, be assertive, and take control of our lives, it's truly freeing.

The way we've viewed ourselves for so long crumbles into a pile of toxic lies fed to us by those who ought to have protected us. It's a bittersweet feeling - more sweet than bitter, though - when we realize we can shed the trauma-induced view of ourselves.

This leads me to the next reason why it's important for you to reconnect with your inner child - **it's empowering**. Little by little, as you add bricks on your path to healing, you'll feel the compound effect of the inner child work you're doing. You'll begin to feel more secure in who you are. You'll begin to understand the dynamic of guilt and shame and know why you felt those things and why you don't need to keep feeling that way. You'll uncover an inner strength you never knew you had. You'll find that you're capable of regulating your emotions.

You may find your values and opinions change or that you can finally muster up the courage to voice them. These things may sound small or humble to other people, but for those of us who've not known the freedom of being able to use our voice, it's nothing short of extraordinary.

The other benefit of reaching out to your inner child is that it enables you to pinpoint and **change any negative behaviors that the trauma triggered.** For example, you may find that when someone gives you feedback or some constructive advice, you get defensive and argumentative. This is because the feedback makes you feel small and stupid, just like you did as a child. Or, if your partner doesn't text you back quickly, you may suddenly feel they don't want to be in the relationship anymore. This is because you felt rejected as a child and are always on high alert for rejection as an adult.

You'll be surprised at the amount of negative, self-sabotaging behaviors you've picked up while trying to avoid being re-traumatized. The ironic thing is, the avoidance of your trauma by using your inner child's coping mechanisms only serves to keep you trapped in the cycle of trauma.

After figuring out why you react to situations in negative ways, you can set about correcting yourself. It's not an overnight fix, and you may have slip-ups along the way, but you'll be on the way to becoming the best version of yourself. And, if you do happen to revert back to your old ways sometimes, remember it's a marathon, not a sprint. You've thought and felt the way you do for so long that who can blame you for defaulting back into that pattern in a tough situation? The important thing is to recognize the regression and move forward.

You may be wondering, *how exactly do I reconnect with my inner child*? Let me show you some techniques. First, imagine there's an invisible string that tethers you and your inner child. The only way to get that invisible rope to glow is by following the techniques I'll discuss now. The more you practice each one and the more consistent you are about carrying out these practices, the more lights will appear on the string. Eventually, you'll have a well-lit tether leading you to "little you" that you can access any time you want. And visa versa: your inner child can reach out to you when they need you, too.

First off, this may sound incredibly obvious, but you need to acknowledge the existence of your inner child. Everyone has an inner child. Every celebrity, every CEO, every single individual on this planet has their younger self inside of them. To most people, they think the reference to their inner child is to refer to their immature, naive self. It's absolutely not the case.

Your inner child is where all your formative thoughts, feelings, events, and emotions are stored. It's so much more than your playful, precocious side. With that said, let's delve into reconnecting with your younger self.

1. Find your inner child

It can be hard to know where to start. Begin by noticing what the children in your life can teach you. Their joy at small things, their wonder at learning new things, and their reaction to things that upset them. Does it take you back to your own childhood? Does it remind you of how you were as a youngster, perhaps during the time in your life when trauma hadn't quite reached you yet?

Use this to rekindle your memories. Do you have any items from your childhood that you can root out? I didn't have much; I didn't have pictures or toys, but I did have an old games console I used to love. My mother had thrown out all my stuffed animals and dolls that I'd collected, but for some reason, I'd managed to keep this old gaming system.

I'd not played video games in years. But, after learning about connecting to my inner child, I decided to head to the loft and dig it out. I managed to find it and could only hope it would work. I didn't have an old enough TV for it to work on, so I even bought one to set it up.

Once I'd plugged it in, inserted a game, and turned it on, I was immediately eight years old again. The comforting sound of the music, the memory of sitting like this in the early 90s, right up close to the TV screen. Behind me on the sofa were my mom and dad, the smell of cigarettes and whisky flooding back to me. The heat from the fire beside me. I felt comfort, something I didn't always associate with my youth.

Of course, other memories came back, too. Like the times I was playing on the console in my bedroom and hitting pause on my game because I could hear my dad beating my mom downstairs. Or my mom threatening to sell the console if I didn't pass an exam. Or playing games with tears streaming down my face because I'd been yelled at for telling my aunt that she was more fun than my mother.

Simply using the game console as a tool ignited so many buried memories and feelings, which led to even more memories and feelings being uncovered. It was in equal parts upsetting, enlightening, comforting, and liberating. I cried and I contemplated as I followed the trail of traumatic events that were suddenly lighting up in my memory, moving from the "suppressed" section to the forefront of my mind.

If you can't obtain anything materialistic from your childhood, then try putting on a TV show or movie from your youth. One that really resonated with you; the type of film that you watched multiple times growing up. Let the movie transport you back to your younger self. Imagine they're sitting on the couch with you, and you're watching it together. Look over to yourself - what are you doing? Are you laughing at certain jokes? Do they still make you laugh now? Tell your younger self so.

Another way you can do this is by revisiting places of significance from your youth. The park near your childhood home. The shopping center your mother used to take you for new school shoes. What about the racetrack your father took you to on a Saturday afternoon? Or drive through the country roads where you would walk the dogs as a child. Have a think, and use what's available to you to reach out to younger you.

Visualization plays a big part here, too. Use the trigger - mine was my games console - and go from there. Sink into old feelings and thoughts.

It's important to note that you won't just return to traumatic events because your childhood wasn't 100% trauma. It can feel that way sometimes, but there are always glimmers of comfort and contentment, even if they didn't last that long. Take the good memories and the bad, and remember, both of them made you who you are today.

I would also suggest engaging in hobbies and activities you enjoyed doing as a child. For me, it was drawing. I was considered quite a good cartoonist growing up, a skill I lost when I stopped drawing around age 12. I would lose myself in recreating the cartoons off the TV or making caricatures of my dog, spending hours detaching myself from the screaming and shouting going on around me by putting pencil to paper.

When I wanted to reach out to my inner child, I bought some coloring pens, pencils, and paper and spent a few hours one afternoon doodling. It reminded me how much I enjoyed it, but it also helped me connect with my inner child. I even began asking my inner child what they thought of my sketches - have we still got the talent? I asked.

Yes, was the obvious reply.

2. Hug your inner child

This may sound woo-woo or unscientific like it did to me when I first heard about "hugging yourself." *How on earth can you possibly do that*? My literal-thinking self questioned.

We need to be open to ways that allow us to heal, even if it means practicing things we don't consider practical or logical. Hugging my inner child sounded off-putting to me. Plus, the younger me wasn't used to hugs, so they probably wouldn't like that, I thought.

What I didn't consider was that my current way of thinking wasn't helping heal my trauma. I needed to be open to new ways of connecting with my inner child and not close myself off from possible healing opportunities. So, I delved into this exercise and learned how to self-soothe by utilizing the "butterfly hug."

Put your left hand on the right side of your chest, just below your collarbone.

Put your right hand on the left side of your chest, just below your collarbone.

Interlock your thumbs - this makes the "butterfly."

Pat gently using one or both hands - see what you find most comforting.

While you're doing this, breathe in deeply through your nose and exhale through your mouth.

Think about all the times during your childhood when you needed comfort. For someone to take you away from the trauma you were enduring and give you a hug. To be offered the safety and warmth of an embrace.

Perhaps it was when your mother was being especially cruel to you. Maybe you witnessed a horrific episode of violence, and nobody consoled you. Maybe it was when a parent blamed you for something you didn't do, and you were punished. Perhaps you're taken back to the time you needed a coat for the harsh winter weather and got frostbite since your parents didn't buy you one.

Take yourself there, to that very moment, and be the comfort you needed back then.

Now would be a good time for you to practice this. Take fifteen minutes, and give it a go. Remember, slow, deep breaths and gentle patting as you imagine yourself embracing your younger self.

3. Do what childhood you couldn't

As a child, I desperately wanted to dress myself. I wasn't allowed to choose my own clothing and wore mostly what my mother chose for me. On the odd occasion, I got to pick my own items of clothing, but very rarely. So, I often found myself in outfits I disliked and was uncomfortable in. I'd given up protesting this with my mother; she'd only make me feel guilty. Plus, she said I looked unattractive in the clothes I wanted to wear so she was doing me a favor.

Naturally, this meant even when I was an adult and could pick my own style, I felt awkward about it. I liked the clothes I was buying, but I still felt uncertain about wearing them. I found myself subconsciously picking out outfits that weren't "me" and were more my mother.

However, when engaging in my inner child work, I knew I needed to fix this. Even in my 30s, I was still conforming to what made my mother happy, not me. I worked hard to resolve this and took my inner child on a shopping trip. It wasn't expensive, just a few slogan tees I knew 11-year-old me would love. I still love them now. It felt comforting and empowering to know I'd made little me and adult me happy by doing something we were never permitted to do.

Try doing something with your inner child that you'd not been allowed to do as a child. It could be getting a meal from a fast food place, staying in your pajamas all day, having cereal for supper, or having dessert before your main course. Whatever it is, do it. There's nobody stopping you now.

4. Find power in the mirror

After enduring a traumatic childhood, we're left filled with an abundance of negative thoughts and feelings toward ourselves. Without really knowing, we think we're not good enough, we aren't important, and we don't matter. These thoughts swirl in our subconscious, having thrived there since we were young.

If you think hard enough about it, do you have any prevailing, persistent negative thoughts about yourself that spill out in the way you talk to yourself?

For example, whenever I used to make a mistake, such as spilling a glass of water, I'd think to myself, "Stupid girl, Kate!" while mopping it up. "Stupid girl," was one of my mother's insults toward me. It then became my own insult toward myself.

I didn't truly realize that until I began taking stock of my inner talk. This is where utilizing your bathroom mirror will help.

You need to make a loving connection with yourself, not be talking to yourself with such disdain and cruelty. Others may have treated you like that in the past, but why are you doing it to yourself now? We need to break out of that negative behavior and begin healing by talking to our mirror reflection and offering them some firm, honest statements. Some examples are:

"I have inner strength."

"I am not my past."

"I matter. What I want matters."

"I am safe."

"Other people's treatment of me does not reflect my value."

You can tailor your statements or affirmations to areas you need to work on. For example, one of mine was, "I am intelligent and thoughtful." These are two things my mother made me believe I wasn't. I was stupid and thoughtless. I made sure my affirmations reminded me I needed to undo the damage her words had done to my inner child and, therefore, me. Of course, sometimes I did feel like a fraud when I stood in front of the mirror, talking to myself. But, remember, our subconscious believes what it's repeatedly fed. Why feed it toxicity when we can now nourish it?

6. Letters to your inner child

I'd tried to journal a little in my 20s, often giving up or putting the notebook in the bin for fear of it being found and all my insecurities being discovered. Plus, I always found myself omitting things just in case someone read it, which was me whitewashing my own experiences.

In my 30s, I tried again, and this time, it morphed into a journal of letters to my childhood self. I even accompanied some with drawings I knew little me would be proud of.

I've selected a few paragraphs that stick with me, and I encourage you to write your own notes for your childhood self.

You were a child; you were powerless to stop the violence and the chaos. You had no control over being there, and you were forced to endure 14 years of horror. Don't ever feel like there was something you could or should have done. You were the child; they were supposed to be the adults.

I know you know no other way, but living in fear isn't living. I know you're afraid and you've based all of our life choices on avoiding pain and rejection, but we don't need to live like that anymore.

We can still love our mother while knowing she failed us and let us down. We don't need to villainize her, but we can still hold her accountable for her actions. Same with dad. I think, sometimes, when we cry over them, we're crying over the parents they weren't - mourning them in a way.

6. Get to know your triggers

What makes you explode with rage? What frustrates you so much that you could cry? What scenarios are you fearful of in life?

For each of these feelings, try to retrace it back to a time in childhood. I used to feel utter rage when I could smell stale alcohol on someone's breath. When my ex would go out with friends and return home drunk, I could smell the alcohol on their breath, and it would take me right back to being a child. I'd be nine years old again, smelling stale booze as my father lay in a heap on the floor, surrounded by scattered pills, cigarette butts, and a pile of his vomit next to him.

The smell would make me so angry that I'd have to sleep in another room to avoid it. For most people, it's just an unpleasant smell that goes away after some mouthwash and toothpaste are used. For me, it would truly cause me to feel intense anger.

Something that I feared for a long time was my partner suddenly deciding they didn't want to be with me. Growing up, I knew how moods and feelings changed. Both of my parents had inconsistent moods; they may wake up angry and full of disdain toward me. But, by afternoon, they may enter my room and give me a candy bar because they "know it's my favorite." I never knew where I stood. So, as an adult, I was always waiting for people to change their minds about me.

This would become especially clear when my partner wouldn't answer my call or take hours to reply to a text. I'd fret and worry that they'd realized I was unworthy and were sick of me.

When you get triggered by something - be it a smell, the way someone talks to you, or something you saw - you need to reach out to your inner child. They were the one who felt these immense feelings first, and you need to remind them that they're safe, you're there to take care of them, and they don't need to live in fear.

You're an adult now, and you are in control. You aren't a powerless child anymore, and these strong emotions don't need to consume you.

Before I end this chapter, I want to make sure that, when you're confronting aspects of your past while connecting with your inner child, that you're in a safe place to do so.

If you're in a bad place emotionally and have extremely negative thoughts about life, you would not be in a safe place to revisit dangerous past experiences. Make sure that you understand it can be emotionally taxing to carry out inner child work in the beginning stages.

You've got this and you'll get there.

Chapter 4: Self-Compassion, Guilt and Shame

Why don't you give yourself the same compassion you give others?

I want to dedicate this whole chapter to a topic about something I bet you rarely offer yourself: compassion. In this section, I want to talk about how self-compassion helps and heals the inner child, how to cultivate it, and how you can break the cycle of feeling shame and guilt.

Some people (my former self included) equate self-compassion to feeling sorry for yourself or leaning into a victim mentality. I can't be further from the truth. After having any notions of self-kindness stomped out of you as a child, it can be hard to engage in self-compassion as an adult. You feel self-centered, egotistical, and self-indulgent for even thinking about it.

What self-compassion really is, is treating yourself with kindness, being supportive toward yourself, and avoiding negative self-talk. You have to treat yourself like a best friend, someone you'd encourage and champion, and have their back no matter what. There are so many people in this world who are quick to mistreat, berate, and put others down. Why would you want to treat yourself this way? You and your inner child are in this for the rest of your life. Why not cultivate a place of kindness and encouragement rather than put yourself down?

Reflect on the opening quote: why *don't* you give yourself the same compassion you give others?

You need to wipe clean everything bad thought about yourself, every insult that's become a persistent toxic thought, and every self-fulfilling prophecy you've thought into existence. Those thoughts and beliefs need to be replaced with self-compassion. Childhood you didn't feel entirely loved or cared for, but you can make sure your inner child doesn't have to keep feeling such negativity and self-loathing by cultivating kindness and love for yourself.

If, as I did, you push back on the idea of engaging in self-compassion (even subconsciously), let me explain why that might be.

You may feel anger and resentment toward your inner child: misplaced feelings to avoid confronting the real traumas of your youth. In this case, there is simply no room for self-compassion. Add to the fact that your poor sense of self is so ingrained that showing yourself some kindness isn't even a consideration.

If you grew up feeling unlovable and unwanted, you may harbor blameful feelings toward yourself: *I was mistreated because I'm hard to love.* The blame and shame of believing this to be true is enough for you to starve yourself of compassion. When we have a distorted view of the world and ourselves, it's understandable that we can also carry a distorted view of the trauma we went through, too.

Still, there's an inner child longing to be cared for and looked after, and the only way you can do this is by shedding the identity the trauma gave you. Once you do this and begin practicing self-compassion, the healing process truly gets its wheels in motion.

Before I explain some exercises that help cultivate self-compassion, I'd just like to note that this isn't a one-and-done thing. You don't just offer yourself some much-needed compassion for a few days and then revert back to your old ways. This is an ongoing thing, something we need to check in on and maintain.

Naturally, there will be times when you regress into old, cruel ways of thinking about yourself. You thought this way for so many years it can be a hard habit to break. But, as long as you recognize this as unhealthy and remind yourself you're working to heal and thrive, you can quickly get yourself back on the right track.

Write a compassionate letter to yourself

This is a bit different from writing letters to your inner child. These are letters of self-compassion to the person you are today.

These letters don't have to be long or wordy, or even on paper. You can use a notes app on your phone or even use a napkin. Just get it out.

You should write a compassionate letter to yourself when you're finding things stressful or you're going through a difficult time. For example, "I know you're feeling like things are rough right now, but you've got this. We've been through worse and we can get through this!"

Longer letters with more depth are always a more introspective way to show yourself compassion. It can help you process the difficult time you're going through while simultaneously letting yourself know you're strong, capable, and deserving of kindness.

Treat yourself as you would a friend who is going through a tough time. Would you tell them to stop being so pathetic? That everything is their own fault? That they deserve every bad thing that comes their way?

Of course you wouldn't. So you certainly shouldn't be talking to yourself that way.

Confront your inner critic

The put-downs, the insults, and the self-deprecating "humor" need to be confronted.

A while ago, I learned a good trick to use when someone was making sarcastic or cruel comments about you in a group setting. I used to have a stereotypical "mean boss" who would throw jibes and snarky remarks in their day-to-day conversation. For example, when one of the girls in the office got her hair colored, he remarked how it "wasn't like her" to make an effort like that. Another time, when we got our bonuses, he told the females not to spend it on shoes. On another occasion, he scolded a worker for the type of clothing she wore into the office - a conversion that ought to have been reserved for a private room, if anywhere at all.

He was a real piece of work, but there was a trick to making him eat his derogatory, snarky, impertinent remarks.

When he said one of his "jokey" jibes, I'd refrain from laughing and act like I didn't quite hear what he said. "I'm sorry - could you repeat that?" I'd ask.

Of course, he'd repeat what he said, but it didn't quite have the same impact since he'd had to say it twice. Once he'd repeated it with a much flatter response, I'd question the comment.

"What do you mean by that?" or, "I don't quite get what you mean; could you explain?"

This would mean he'd have to dissect his comment in front of other people and inadvertently expose it as the cruel remark it was intended to be. Not to mention, it made him feel stupid for saying it - as it should. He used put-downs to make himself feel bigger. Bullying tactics, essentially.

I'm telling you this because that's how I want you to confront your own inner bully. The critic that ebbs away at any confidence or esteem that may rise up. The toxic inner dialogue that treats you like you're worthless. Stand up to them.

Ask them - *you* - to repeat what they've said.

Question it. Why? Why did they say that, why do they think that's appropriate, and what was the desired outcome of the comment?

You'll soon realize that you're wildly unfair and unkind to yourself a lot of the time. Stop the inner critic in their tracks. More often than not, they're not trying to stop you from embarrassing yourself or doing something you're incapable of; they're making you regress to childhood you.

The difference is that when you were younger, you didn't have the courage to stand up for yourself. You didn't have someone standing in your corner to have your back and save you. Now you do: adult you.

Check-in with yourself

Often, we simply need to take a break, gather our thoughts, and check in with ourselves. Have we been too harsh on ourselves lately? Have we been full of judgment, blame, and frustration and aiming it toward ourselves? Sometimes, we can be incredibly tough on ourselves when what we need is calmness, room for better thinking, and some reassurance. We can't be our best selves when we're forever berating ourselves.

At the end of every day, while you're trying to fall asleep, think about how you've treated yourself that day. Were you patient with yourself? If you could have been better in a particular situation, did you remind yourself of this in a kind, encouraging way? Did you remember to correct yourself for any toxic thoughts?

Doing this at the end of the day allows for a clear overview of how you treated yourself on that day. It also means that the last thing you thought about before you drifted off was how you can be more compassionate with yourself. Without you knowing, this will seep into your subconscious.

Be forgiving

Childhood trauma breeds persistent feelings of guilt, shame, and blame. Nothing we did as a child could ever be something we ought to feel guilt over. Sometimes, though, the effects of childhood trauma can cause adult us to behave in ways that are undesirable.

We may find we're quick to insult someone when they inadvertently offend us. We may choose to ghost a love interest when they upset us instead of talking over our concerns. We may start an argument when things are going "too well." Our knee-jerk reactions to certain situations is a result of our childhood, and although we may feel bad and damaged for behaving that way, we need to offer ourselves more forgiveness.

You've acknowledged your actions weren't great - that's a brilliant starting point. Most people never realize their transgression and, therefore, never correct it. You're in a position to learn from your mistakes and correct them. While you may beat yourself up, be full of judgment for yourself, and be internally cursing yourself for your difficult behavior, don't get hung up on being so harsh.

We can't change the past; we can only learn from it. If you can be better moving forward, then you have to forgive yourself and work towards betterment. Apologize where necessary, hold yourself accountable, learn from your mistakes, and forgive yourself.

Seek out common ground with others

Too often, our go-to coping mechanism is to retreat and cut off other people. People were the source of our trauma, and people can exacerbate that trauma. Sometimes, the only option we feel we have is to be alone.

This isn't the case.

Finding a connection with others is fantastic medicine for a wounded inner child. Don't shy away from others, don't avoid making connections for fear of being hurt, and open yourself up a little.

This doesn't just pertain to in-person connections. When I first began seeking out guidance to heal my hurt inner child, my search began online. I found forums and groups dedicated to healing from childhood trauma, and a whole new world opened up before me. Here, there were people who'd been through similar things to me, people who'd healed from the trauma, and others who were behind me in the healing process. Regardless, each person either had something to teach me or offered me comfort that I wasn't alone. More than that, I didn't need to be alone in order to protect myself.

It can be easier to open up emotionally online, but eventually, some of these internet friends can become genuine friends. I've made a few friends throughout my healing journey simply by seeking out people who were similar to me. Being able to talk about events and feelings without feeling judged or disbelieved was inexplicably empowering.

Cultivate acceptance (even for your flaws)

We've been trained to dislike ourselves, creating cognitive dissonance and inner turmoil as we grew up. We need to accept ourselves, flaws and all, before we can truly heal. Are we perfect? There's no such thing. Are we trying to better ourselves and our lives and cultivate a better world around us? Absolutely.

Accept your limitations just as much as your capabilities. Embrace them, acknowledge them, celebrate them, and accept them.

I've talked about guilt and shame. No doubt, like so many of us with wounded inner children, you understand the heavy weight of living with immense guilt and shame. In this next section, I want to cover how you can begin eroding the persistent feelings of negativity you have toward yourself, beginning with guilt and shame.

You need to let your inner child know that they can let go of these feelings. Once they do, you'll be able to drop them too.

Tell your inner child that you **hear them.** Do you remember being upset about something as a child and being unheard when you sought comfort or reassurance? Or that your crying was labeled an annoyance and your needs were dismissed? *"You can see I'm busy. Go away,"* or *"You're not upset, stop acting like the victim."* Phrases like this stick with a child.

This means, that as an adult, we tend to act tougher than we are. We absorb pain and upset and don't open up about it.

You know that's no good for you or your inner child. You need to let younger you know that their feelings are heard, that they are heard. When you get pangs of upset or hurt, remind your inner child that you're there and that you hear them. Tell them it's going to be okay - offer them the words of comfort you ought to have had as a child. No more suppression for you or the child within.

Remind younger you that they in no way deserved the trauma they endured. **"You didn't deserve that"** may be a simple sentence, but it goes a long way for your inner child. You weren't bad, unlovable, an annoyance, stupid, a mistake, or any other horrible thing you were led to believe you were. Those traumatic words weren't a reflection of you. They were certainly a reflection of the person who said them. The distressing situations you were put in as a child weren't a reflection of you. They, too, were a reflection of the person who put you in them. And you didn't deserve to go through any of that. No child does.

What is more innocent than a child? They are brand new to the world, trying to figure it out and understand it. The caregiver's role is to guide them not to scold them for not knowing. As a child, we simply didn't have the capacity to understand that things weren't our fault. But, now we do, let's let our inner child know that.

"I'm sorry you went through that" is a much-needed but often neglected phrase for your inner child.

Forgive yourself for any childhood behaviors that still irk you. For example, telling parents you hate them or any childhood fibs you may have told. When my mother and father separated in my late teens, my father told me it was because of my wayward teenage behavior. Staying out, drinking, and having a bad attitude. They simply couldn't take my selfish behavior, and I had ruined their relationship.

For years, I carried this burden with me. I truly believed I had been the one to end a relationship of 25 years. I hated myself for that, and I cringed at my reckless, selfish teenage action that led to the end of my parent's marriage.

In reality, I had nothing to do with the breakdown of the relationship. It was the decades of domestic abuse, alcohol abuse, emotional abuse, and emotional immaturity that the relationship was built around. My mother had simply had enough. My father couldn't accept his role in this, so he blamed me. In turn, I blamed myself. I fell into a very dark place after this.

Only after working to heal my traumas and after his death did I come to realize it had nothing to do with me. I had to learn to forgive myself.

You also need to **remind your inner child that you appreciate them.** *I don't appreciate them holding on to years of trauma*, you may be thinking to yourself (remember, your inner child is privy to your thoughts, too!)

Look at it in a more compassionate, understanding way. Your inner child held onto all that trauma and misery to protect you. To stop you from having to endure the same pain as they did. Do you remember the first time you felt shame or deep rejection? Your inner child was holding on to those memories to make sure you never felt that gut-wrenching heartbreak ever again.

Your inner child endured trauma and emotional injury so that you could be here today. Tell them you appreciate them. They're stronger than they ever realized.

Not only that, remind them that **they did their best** with the knowledge and abilities they had. You were a child. You didn't know how to stick up for yourself, how to navigate being blamed for something you didn't do, how to deal with the pain of being treated unfairly, or how to process being abused. And, still, here you are: you got through it despite the damage you endured.

To draw this chapter to a close, I want you to take some time to consider this question. Everyone's answer is different because everyone's experience of trauma is different. What one thing would you like your inner child to know that they couldn't possibly have known as a child?

While you take some time to answer this question, here is a reminder of the things you need to tell your wounded inner child:

I hear you

You didn't deserve that

I'm sorry you went through that

I forgive you

I appreciate you

You did your best

I don't need to tell you that one of the biggest obstacles to overcome when healing your inner child is fixing how you talk to yourself. Remedy that by regularly referring to the above affirmations and passing them on to your inner child.

Chapter 5: Untangle Limiting Beliefs

You can't escape from prison when you don't realize you're in one.

A limiting belief is a belief about yourself that restricts you. This belief is your truth; it's a fact. For example, one of my limiting beliefs was that I was anti-social. What caused me to think that way? And why did that thought stick around for so long?

Growing up, I'd avoid having friends over to stay at the house. I'd avoid going to classmates' birthday parties. I'd stay in my room when family members came to visit. I'd keep away from any kind of attention, good or bad, and try to minimize my presence by blending into the backdrop. Because of this, my mother would often call me "anti-social" or "miserable."

The "anti-social" habits I picked up as a child often exhibited themselves in adulthood, too. I'd say no to co-workers who invited me to after-work drinks. I'd let other people at work take credit for my efforts since I preferred to stay out of the spotlight. I went through a phase of saying I had plans on a weekend to avoid making plans on a weekend.

I'm just anti-social, I thought to myself.

I simply accepted that label and ran with it. Never had I considered what the term actually meant: *acting in a way that causes annoyance and disapproval in others.*

My mother called me anti-social, but I wasn't. Perhaps, to her, I was. After all, I rarely got her approval and always seemed to annoy her. But, I really wasn't anti-social. Not in the true sense of the term. What child is? What happy, nurtured, curious child is anti-social?

The reason I exhibited behaviors she labeled as this was because of her and my father. I'd avoid having classmates come to the house because I was afraid of them seeing how I lived. My father was a bumbling drunk, and my mother made the atmosphere tense and anxious. I didn't go to birthday parties because the stress of having to pay for the birthday gift would make my mother upset. I'd stay away from family members who visited the home in case I said something to them that would upset my mother. Like the time I told an uncle about a toy I really wanted but I didn't think Santa would bring it because there wasn't enough money. I got screamed at for that once my uncle left.

So, I retreated away from people and scenarios that would cause upset and confrontation. In doing so, I became "anti-social," as my mother would tell people. In reality, I was a scared, anxious, people-pleasing child who just wanted love and calmness. I did what I thought I had to in order to obtain that.

Our belief systems are set up from us being very small children. These beliefs stay with us as we grow, and we lean into them, creating events, scenarios, and experiences that affirm these beliefs to be true. We become that self-fulfilling prophecy.

We are fueled and navigated by our beliefs. If we believe we can do something, we'll put ourselves out there and do what it takes to reach our goal. Be it career, relationship, or even materialistic goals, if we think we can, we'll most likely do whatever we need to get there. Similarly, if we think we can't, we can't. Not due to lack of capabilities or because we're not good enough - but because our negative belief system discourages us. It tells us we can't, and we believe that.

Limiting beliefs are everywhere, and people often expose theirs if you're listening hard enough. I had an old boss who once asserted that, biologically, men will always be more attracted to younger women. "Women mature more quickly," he'd argue if one of the girls questioned this belief. He truly believed that men in their 50s, like he was, would never date within their own age range.

The more I thought about this, the more I wondered where this limiting belief came from. I don't actually have the answer, but I did spend time pondering. Could he be intimidated by women who are older and who have life experience and are more likely to have boundaries? Was his father much older than his mother? The reasons for his limiting belief were endless, but they stemmed from somewhere, likely in childhood.

Another example is from a former co-worker. A project manager job came up, and we were both project assistants. She'd been there longer than me and would have flourished if she got that role. "I'm too old to apply now. They want younger, trendier people for that job." They didn't. I knew they didn't, but I couldn't convince my competent co-worker otherwise. Naturally someone else got the job, but my friend's limiting belief cost her the opportunity to even try. Her insistence that her age was a barrier was one she placed there herself.

Again, we can never know where other people's limiting beliefs come from - almost always childhood, though - but we can figure out where ours stemmed. Sometimes we can even pinpoint the event that spawned the limiting belief.

First, have a think about some of your inner dialogue that can lead you to an inner belief. They can often be disguised as mere thoughts, like, "I'm so unlucky." This automatically becomes your excuse if things don't work out or is your reason for not stepping out of your comfort zone. Another could be, "I'm a slow learner." We all process and digest things at our own pace, but if you tell yourself you're a slow learner, that's what you'll be.

Once you've identified some of your limiting beliefs, you need to ask yourself why you feel that belief to be true. Trace it back as far as you can. My guess is that, more often than not, you'll be guided back to childhood.

Take a few moments to pinpoint and find the source of some of your limiting beliefs. Once you have, we can move on to banishing them. I'll be ready to continue when you are. Grab a pen and paper, too.

Write the limiting beliefs down

It's great you've picked up on some of your limiting beliefs and recognized them for what they are. It's hard for us to disbelieve something after we've thought it to be the truth for so long. To get that negative pattern of thinking out of your head, I find it a good exercise to write them down. It feels like you're literally removing them from your brain and disposing of them on paper.

I know it's not as easy as that, but it's a mental technique that helps cement in your mind that these thoughts are false limitations imposed on us by the traumas we endured.

You may think to yourself, *I have this belief about myself because it's true.* I am insecure, quiet, socially awkward, absent-minded, or whatever limiting belief you have. You may even be able to think of some examples of times you have been those things.

But why are you arguing in favor of your limitations? From past events, I could have probably successfully argued that my mother was right about me being anti-social. I avoided being in social settings.

But I wasn't anti-social, I was made that way due to my surroundings.

Belief does not equate truth

Some people think the earth is flat. Some people believe microwaves cause incurable diseases. Some people think dinosaurs never existed. Some people believe that lightning can't strike in the same place twice.

My point is that a strongly held belief doesn't equal the truth. Not to say the above beliefs are wrong - we all have our own ideologies and credences - but it points out just how much power a strongly held belief can have.

Assess your limiting thoughts and beliefs, weed them out, and truly question their legitimacy. Remember, if you fight for them, they're yours. Be picky about what you choose to keep.

Accept beliefs can change

When you uncover some beliefs that you accept aren't truths, you then need to be open to changing that belief.

For example, when I threw out my long-held view that I was anti-social, I replaced it with the truth: that I was a contemplative and thoughtful person who could sometimes be introverted. However, I am friendly, welcoming, and empathetic towards others, a stark contrast to the "anti-social" label I held onto for so long.

Go through your self-limiting thoughts and rewire them.

Maybe you say to yourself, "I'm always broke because I'm not good with money." Replace that with, "I've been through financial struggles and I'm learning to deal with my finances better."

Use your pen and paper to write your new truths next to your old beliefs. Read it aloud. Repeat it to yourself. Remind yourself why you thought so negatively in the first place and why you're doing the work to fix that.

Change your behavior

Step one is acknowledging your limiting beliefs, pinpointing their source, and then rewiring them. Step two is ensuring your new beliefs - your new truths - are reflected in your behavior.

For example, if you've always thought you weren't bright enough to pursue your dream career, what can you do to align with your new truth? For me, I never thought I'd be able to pursue a career in journalism. I would scroll the social media of the girls I went to high school with and see them excel in their high-paying positions while I was still in my hometown working a menial job. I wasn't good enough to be like them I thought.

Until in my 30s, I began addressing my traumas and unhealed childhood wounds. Within six months of this, I was attending night classes, submitting my work to local publishers, and taking the steps I needed to in order to pursue my dream career.

The beliefs that I wasn't good enough and not smart enough had held me back for so long. It wasn't enough to just acknowledge I'd been living with limiting beliefs, I had to put in the work to rewire my brain from thinking them.

The piece of paper you use to note down all your limiting beliefs - keep it if you can. You'll likely need to add to it as you continue your healing journey. Subconscious limiting beliefs can pop up from out of nowhere, and we had no idea it was an untruth born out of someone else's idea of us. Add it to your list, write your new truth next to it, and remember to put your new belief into action.

Chapter 6: Nurture Your Inner Child

What do you do when your inner child wants love, your inner teen wants revenge, but the adult you wants calmness and peace?

What do you think the answer to that question is? Childhood trauma can cause so many conflicting and contradictory feelings to swirl inside of you. How do you find a resolution that's best for you and soothes your inner child?

It's a process called re-parenting.

Being the parent you needed doesn't just mean being the nurturing and supportive caregiver you should have had. It also means incorporating all the "boring" parental aspects, such as consistency, discipline, and ensuring you're taken care of.

As an adult, you need to establish all the ways you were let down in your youth and endeavor to introduce them into your habits. But how do you do this?

First of all, **respect your childhood feelings**. Connecting with your inner child isn't just about identifying the feelings you harbor, but also validating them. Letting childhood you know that what they felt about and their response to trauma is entirely understandable. When these feelings resurface as an adult, you also need to remind yourself that these emotions are understandable. Naturally, children have a limited capacity for processing traumas and negative emotions. Grown up you now has the ability to deal with childhood emotions in a healthy, compassionate way.

Secondly, you should **remain patient with yourself**. For me, patience was never something I was offered as a child and was, therefore, something I never offered myself as an adult. However, the foundations of good parenting lie within the ability to remain patient and understanding. When we re-parent ourselves, we need to recognize that we've likely carried over our parent's intolerance of us into our own subconscious.

This will likely have affected many aspects of your life. Relationships, career goals, and how we view ourselves overall. Recognize the pattern of your lack of patience with yourself and, moving forward, refrain from being so curt and hasty in your treatment of yourself. It took you years of maltreatment and emotional turmoil to build your self-perception; it's not going to evaporate overnight. But, by recognizing the patterns, you can slowly begin to eradicate them and replace them with a healthier way of treating yourself.

Another main aspect of being a healthy parent is **remaining consistent**. Growing up, did you feel like you were on eggshells, unsure of what mood your parents may be in? Did you find it difficult to gauge what their reactions would be in certain situations? Would they laugh at your behavior one moment and then scold you for the same behavior the next? That's because your caregivers were inconsistent with you.

Naturally, inconsistent parenting leads to an anxious, nervous child who's unsure of what moves to make and how to act in order to please those around them. This unhealthy way of thinking follows the child with them as they grow up. Now you're in a position to re-parent, you need to reassure your inner child of your capabilities by remaining consistent.

If you find yourself slipping in your consistency, be graceful with yourself: you're working to rewire your damaged way of thinking. It won't all come together overnight. Acknowledge that you regressed to your former pattern of thinking, and move forward.

All of this: having to rewire your thinking patterns, revisiting old, traumatic memories, and working to fix your negative self-talk can be overwhelming. When you feel you're drowning or lost in your healing journey, you need to ask yourself one question: why?

Remind yourself why you're doing this. Re-parenting yourself wouldn't be necessary if you'd had a healthy, nurturing upbringing. Remind yourself of your why. This will help you find your way again and show you why you started this process.

Discipline is a word that can evoke feelings of terror and unease. However, true parental discipline isn't scary or fear-inducing. It's nourishing guidance, a gentle reminder of right and wrong, and instills your moral compass. As an adult, you need to **embrace self-discipline.**

You may think you were disciplined as a child. Shouting and punishments don't equate true discipline. Structure in your life: set bedtimes, routine, explaining why it's not okay to act out, calm consequences, and nonviolent correction are all discipline. How many of those did you receive?

When we are disciplined incorrectly, we struggle to hold ourselves accountable as adults. Remember that you can and should be practicing self-discipline. Your inner child needs that kind of stability.

Another thing re-parenting requires is for you to remember to **be curious and seek out joy**. Do you remember laughing at something as a child or being intrigued by something that awed you? Did your caregiver slap that joyful moment away from you or prevent you from exploring that joy further?

For example, on my way to school, we would pass a field of cows. One day, one of them was scratching its face on the fencepost, and I giggled at the sight. I'd never seen a cow scratching its itch before, nor did I realize they got itchy. *How clever is that cow*, I thought to myself. When my mother caught me laughing, she told me to stop being so stupid and infantile. When I then asked questions about cows, I was told I asked the most ridiculous questions.

Of course cows get itchy! You really are stupid; I have no idea why you ask such dumb questions.

Naturally, I felt utterly embarrassed and brainless. Interactions like this compounded, and eventually, my wonder and curiosity were stomped out.

As an adult, it's your duty to your inner child to reignite your search for joy and wonder in all the world has to offer.

During your journey toward healing, it's imperative you **avoid basking in blame**. It can be so easy to hold on to blame and resentment. Whether or not your parents hold themselves accountable for their treatment of you as a child is irrelevant. It can, of course, help us on our healing journey if our caregivers hold their hands up to their shortcomings while we were growing up. However, don't base your ability to heal on something you may never get from your parents. You don't need their accountability to find closure or heal your wounds.

You can hold them accountable without holding onto blame. You may have little or no contact with your parents. You may have cut your entire family off, or you may still retain a full relationship with them. No matter your situation, you need to drop the bitterness of blame from your internal monologue.

There's a difference between holding someone accountable for their actions and harboring resentment for their actions. The former allows you to heal; the latter stops you from doing so.

You aren't avoiding feelings of blame for them; you're doing it for you.

As a reminder, here are the key areas to focus on when re-parenting:

Respect your childhood feelings

Remain patient with yourself

Remain consistent

Remind yourself why you're doing this

Embrace self-discipline

Be curious and seek out joy

Avoid basking in blame

Another thing we weren't taught by our parents was boundaries.

Healthy boundaries = healthy life, right?

But what if your boundaries have never been considered, or any boundaries you tried to implement were trod on? What if you were taught that you shouldn't have boundaries or you'll upset other people? The phrase, *you set yourself alight just to keep others warm,* comes to mind.

The purpose of boundaries is to protect us. This makes it easy to realize, then, that the only people who have an issue with us having them are the very people who benefit from us not having any.

So, what is a good example of a boundary? One of my boundaries is that I have alone time. I enjoy reading, so I have a few evenings a week where I'll get lost in a book for a few hours. I will not let people guilt trip me into spending time with them or make me feel bad for wanting some time to destress. The former me would struggle with this. I'd cave so easily if someone made me feel bad. "No" didn't mean no because I'd give in so quickly if someone made me feel guilty for trying to assert my needs.

Our boundaries are our values. I value my time alone. I value being respected. I value being able to be vulnerable around people without shame. I value the ability to have an opinion without fear of rebuttal.

When we don't have boundaries, we are in a persistent state of being unsafe and undefended to the predators of this world. As a child, being boundary-less served a purpose: it stopped adults from being mad at us. It prevented arguments. It stopped our caregivers from disliking us. It helped make the atmosphere calm and dampen the likelihood of danger.

As an adult, it serves no purpose but for those willing to take advantage of your lack of boundaries. You need boundaries in adulthood.

Now you're grown, you can explore your needs and discover your identity without that ever-present danger stopping you from doing so. It can be hard to convince yourself of this. We've been in fight, flight or freeze for so long, simply getting by in survival mode. But we have to learn we don't need to endure life this way. We can live life if we begin to take control of it. We can't control other people, but we can control ourselves and how we react to maltreatment.

Here are some examples of poor boundaries as a result of unresolved childhood trauma:

You find it hard to say "no." No matter how much you want to say no, you simply can't. The person requesting something of you will dislike you or begin to resent you. Simply put your fragile sense of self couldn't accept that. So, you say "yes" despite it being the opposite of what you want to say. After all, you have to take care of other people's needs and wants before your own. There is less conflict that way.

You find it hard to make decisions because you don't have your own thoughts or opinions to guide you. You're used to implementing others' ideas and desires while neglecting your own, so when it comes to making a choice of your own, you freeze.

Relationships can often feel like a one-way road. You put in the effort, the care, and the thought, but it's not entirely reciprocated. You may find you're the one who arranges dates or meet-ups, and they never plan anything with you. You're the one reaching out with texts and calls. You seem to be the one buying gifts yet rarely receive any. The big thing here is that, even though you're not getting what you truly want out of these relationships, you stay nonetheless.

Other people's moods affect yours. If someone is less chatty or seems a bit low, you feel responsible for that. Often, you might even feel blamed for their mood despite not having any idea what you could have done to cause it. This, as you know, stems from childhood and never being able to appease our caregivers. Often, we'd find them in a foul mood, and they'd take their frustrations out on us. No wonder we feel responsible for others' emotions and moods. *If they're happy, we can be happy,* is a way of thinking that follows us from childhood experiences, as is our willingness to accept blame for other people's temper.

People find they can take advantage of your kindness. For example, people think they can "borrow" something from you but never seem to give it back. This can often be things like money, and these vulture-like individuals know you won't confront them about it.

Let me guide you through the type of boundaries there are to help you build your own.

There are **physical boundaries**. These boundaries dictate how much time you're willing to give someone, how much of your personal space you're comfortable allowing others in, and how tactile you allow others to be with you. It's affirming how ready you are for physical intimacy in a relationship (if at all), and it's being able to set out how you allow others to step into your private spaces, i.e., your bedroom or your home.

This type of boundary keeps you safe in a healthy way. From dealing with strangers to members of your family, if you firmly assert your boundaries, everyone knows where they stand. If someone gets upset with you for putting boundaries in place, you have to ask yourself why that would be.

Then, there are **emotional boundaries**. These help you draw a line where you want to avoid certain conversational topics (such as intimacy or money) or setting out what is acceptable to talk about. This means you stop accepting insults as "jokes" and refuse to engage in topics you've asserted you don't wish to discuss. The main thing you need to remember is that you actually need to set out these boundaries. Yes, in an ideal world, we wouldn't need to warn people that it's inappropriate to comment on our weight or career. However, if you're dealing with narcissistic parents or toxic people, these things need to be laid out clearly.

I implemented a three-strike rule after I asserted my boundaries. Once is a mistake - old habits die hard, and I remind the offender of my boundary. If they do it again, I give them the benefit of the doubt that they won't cross the line again. "I will leave if you ask me that again. I have told you I don't want to talk about that. Can we move on to a different topic?" offers candor in your boundary setting. Should it happen a third time, again, I remind them of the previously laid out boundaries, and I remove myself from their life. Some people may think this is harsh; others may think three chances are two too many; you need to go with what works for you. Remember - you are not responsible for other people's feelings, especially when you've tried so hard to work with that person to create a level playing field of respect.

Sexual boundaries are another extremely important thing to implement. No means no, and you stick to that - there is no three-strike rule for this one. Ever. Conversational slip-ups about money and weight can happen - sexual "slip-ups'" do not. You communicate your boundaries and preferences, and they are to be followed, likewise for you toward your partner.

Financial boundaries refer to money, material items, your car... anything of value that belongs to you. Again, abusers can sense the vulnerable side of a traumatized person and use their kind, passive nature to their own nefarious advantage. They might ask for money or a place to stay or to borrow your vehicle. You'll never see the money again, you don't receive rent for the room you let out, nor do you get your car back when you need it. This is abuse. Set out your financial boundaries clearly. No is a full sentence. When someone asks for money, we often find we scramble for excuses: "I'm so sorry, I have no spare cash this month. The car needed to go to the garage, and the cat needed to go to the vets..." Why can't you just say no? We don't need to offer an explanation. You may equate this to being rude or curt. But consider why you're offering an explanation; you feel guilty for not handing the money over. Guilt is a learned feeling, and you need to work on filtering out your reactions to certain situations.

Your **time boundaries** are often overlooked but are still highly important to you in maintaining a healthy sense of self. If your boss is requesting you work late but you have already planned a trip to the cinema, or if your mother made an appointment for you without your blessing, or if your friend is insisting you go out with them that night, these are all examples of people not acknowledging your time boundaries. More often than not, this is because you've never had them, and you've always just been "available" when people wanted to pick you up and use your time. Consider what your time boundaries are and begin implementing them in your life.

Nurturing your inner child takes time, patience, and work, but the act of reconnecting with little you and helping them heal has untold benefits for present and future you. So many people simply put a band-aid over their inner child's wounds, which solves nothing and exacerbates everything. The fact that you're reading this book and looking to work on healing your painful childhood trauma means you're getting to the source of the agony and exorcizing it from you. For that reason alone, you should be proud of how far you've come despite the roadblocks that have been in your way.

Chapter 7: Letting Go

Letting go of trauma doesn't mean the pain didn't exist or that it vanished from our memory. It just means it no longer controls us.

There's a phrase: you don't forgive for the person you hurt you; you forgive so you can heal. It's true. By forgiving, you're clearing them out of the space they took in your head and making room for healthy, happier thoughts.

You have to remember nobody can heal you except you. Remember: the wounds you have are not your fault. But they are your responsibility to heal.

Resentment doesn't hurt the person who hurt you; it just hurts you. I harbored a tonne of resentment toward my mother and father for years. I had them in my life but had a complex relationship with them. I still desired to please them and make them proud, but I was also bitter and angry toward them. This cognitive dissonance is just unhealthy. There are two options: forgiveness or remaining hurt. Even if going no contact is best for you, you still need to invite forgiveness into your soul in order to heal.

Forgiving doesn't mean you're saying it's okay that they hurt and traumatized you. It means you're saying you're doing what you need to in order to heal. Forgiving does not mean condoning. You are refusing to let the past operate the present.

Let me offer you some guidance on forgiving even when you feel like forgiveness simply isn't possible.

Get another piece of paper and a pen. Let's get the resentment from your head onto paper. I want you to begin the first sentence with "I have resented..." and I want you to fill out the rest.

Mine looked like this:

I have resented you, mom, for all of the hurtful, cruel things you called me growing up. For making me feel shame and embarrassment for just being me. For using me as your personal punching bag, seemingly without any guilt. Rarely did you say sorry for all the nights you sent me to bed in tears for nothing. For the slaps across the face for crying. For the time I overheard you telling dad that I was a mistake. For making me feel so worthless and void of anything good that I spent my first 30 years not wanting to be here.

I have resented you, dad, for making me witness you in frighteningly drunken states. For making me wake up to mom's blood all over the kitchen and her eyes all cut because you punched her glasses into her face. For the time I had to watch her face turn purple because you strangled her so much. For the first and only time you punched me for no reason - I thought I was safe from your beatings, but that time proved I had to be wary around you, too.

Get it all out. Everything you have spent years resenting, pour it out onto the paper. Once you're done - it can be pages if needed, the above paragraphs are merely paragraphs from mine - draw a line under it. Then, write beneath it, "Moving forward, for my own self-care, I will not be keeping this resentment within me."

What you do with this piece of paper is up to you. I kept mine in a drawer I rarely opened. When I discovered it years later, I read it, and it didn't upset me like it would have done years earlier. I had done a lot of healing since I wrote it. I tore it up and put it in the fire. It was kind of ceremonial; truly releasing these feelings and moving forward.

When you feel lost or full of resentment, remember this: you don't choose trauma. But you do choose change.

While you move forward in your healing journey, you will see positive change emanating from the traumas you've endured. This is something called post-traumatic growth. The term was coined in the 90s by psychologists Richard Tedeschi and Lawrence Calhoun. In a nutshell, it is a term to describe the positive psychological change that can occur in individuals after they've endured trauma. Please know that this phenomena doesn't diminish the distress and heartache trauma causes, but points toward the unintentional way it forges good traits in you. Tedeschi and Calhoun found there was five main sectors of growth that occur in some people after trauma:

Changes in how the individual relates to other people

Recognition of new priorities

Greater appreciation for the value of life

The ability to recognize one's own strength

Spiritual or existential growth

When you're in the midst of trauma or have not long escaped from a traumatic situation, naturally, you don't feel any of the above. You feel full of rage, resentment, fear, uncertainty, and heartbreak.

Post-traumatic growth is the very human way of making sense of the trauma, allowing healing to thrive, and using your hardships to learn valuable life lessons. After a crisis, growth can happen. It's important to note that there is no set "timeline" after trauma, nor is there a timeframe in which you go from wounded to healed. Some people, those who don't work on their traumas, never do. But, at some point through this journey, you'll begin to notice growth. In fact, other people may be able to point it out before you've even noticed for yourself. Either way, there will be flowers blooming in a place that was inhabitable before. There will be growth in you that simply wasn't there before.

You may start developing a newfound way of looking at life, appreciating things you didn't notice before. You may find your relationships with others deepens. You might start being more self-reliant emotionally. You may begin to gain clarity on a faith that wasn't there before or have more understanding of a faith you hold.

Post-traumatic growth is only obtained when you acknowledge what happened to you, accept the traumatic events that happened, and are open to healing from them. As I said earlier, you don't choose trauma, but you do choose change.

Thank you for reading *Your Hurt Inner Child*. Although it's a heavy topic, I'm glad you're here - it means you're on your healing journey. You're enlightened to the fact that your inner child needs you, and you're doing the work to figure out how you can heal. Most people never figure out the key to easing their pain and anguish was inside them all along. Granted, the source of the pain and anguish was also inside them all along, but the inner child can't be blamed for their reactions to life's stresses.

As I said in the beginning, *the wounds you have are not your fault. But they **are** your responsibility to heal.*

I truly hope this book has given you food for thought, the desire to cultivate self-compassion and inner kindness, and the knowledge that healing is not just attainable; it's imperative.

I'd like to end this book with a message to your inner child:

You are heard, you are loved, and you will heal.

Quotes from this book followed by quotes that helped me find and heal my inner child:

The wounds you have are not your fault. But they are your responsibility to heal.

Every time I hear someone raising their voice, I regress into six-year-old me.

It's an overwhelming thought to think of how many broken children are suffering inside adult bodies.

How would you take care of little you if you could parent them?

Why don't you give yourself the same compassion you give others?

You can't escape from prison when you don't realize you're in one.

What do you do when your inner child wants love, your inner teen wants revenge, but the adult you wants calmness and peace?

Letting go of trauma doesn't mean the pain didn't exist or that it vanished from our memory. It just means it no longer controls us.

You don't choose trauma, but you do choose change.

Nobody can heal you except you

Even when the conscious mind doesn't have the words to talk about it, the body remembers trauma.

Don't be ashamed of the trauma you've been through. Instead, be proud of how far you've come.

If you refuse to address your trauma, you only wind up bleeding on the people who didn't cut you.

Trauma isn't just a memory; it's a reaction.

You are not defined by your past.